NFT & CRYPTOART

The Complete Guide To Successfully Invest In, Create And Sell Non-Fungible Tokens In The Digital Art Market

Daniel L. Bray

Page intentionally left blank

TABLE OF CONTENTS

INTRODUCTION

NFTs are causing a stir in the art and gaming worlds, so what are they? You may have recently seen the word NFT in the news, often in connection with large amounts of money. However, you might be wondering what all the fuss is about.

This guide will help you understand what an NFT or non-fungible token is and how they function. It will teach you everything you need to know about NFTs, including what they are, how they operate, why they've sparked debate, and how you can help.

An NFT is a non-financial transaction. In essence, an NFT is a collectible digital asset with monetary value. Like architecture, NFTs are now regarded as a long-term investment.

NFT stands for a non-fungible token, a digital token similar to Bitcoin or Ethereum, a form of cryptocurrency. However, unlike a regular Bitcoin coin, an NFT is one-of-a-kind and cannot be traded for another (hence, non-fungible).

NFTs can be anything from digital artwork to a music file, anything original that can be stored digitally and considered valuable. They work similarly to any other physical collector's piece, but instead of an oil painting on canvas to hang on your wall, you get a JPG file.

NFTs are individual tokens that are part of the Ethereum, blockchain, and contaalsoal data. The important part is the extra material, which enables them to be portrayed as art, music, video (and so on) in JPGs, MP3s, images, GIFs, and other formats. They can be purchased and sold like other forms of art because they have value primarily determined by market and demand, much like physical art.

That isn't to suggest that there is only one digital edition of an NFT art on the market. Copies of NFTs are still legitimate parts of the blockchain, much as art prints of originals are made, used, purchased, and sold. However, they may not have the same value as the original.

Don't think that by right-clicking and saving an NFT picture, you've hacked the system. Since your downloaded file does not contain the details that make it part of the Ethereum blockchain, you will not become a millionaire. Does that make sense?

NFTs can be purchased on some sites, depending on what you're looking for (for example, if you're looking for baseball cards, you can go to a site like digital trading cards but other marketplaces offer more generalized items). You'll need a wallet that's unique to the platform you're buying on and cryptocurrencies to place in it.

Some pieces are starting to appear at more mainstream auction houses, so keep an eye out for these as well. Many forms of NFT are often published as 'drops' due to high demand (much like in events, when batches of tickets are often released at different times).

This means that there will be a frantic rush of hopeful customers when the drop begins, so be sure to register and get your wallet filled up ahead of time.

NFTs are also becoming common as in-game purchases in various video games. Players can buy and sell these properties, including playable items such as exclusive swords, skins, and avatars.

NFTs are certainly having a moment, with artists, gamers, and brands from all walks of life contributing to the trend. In reality, it appears that a new player joins the NFT market every day. Are you ready to explore it?

Let's get the ball rolling.

CHAPTER 1

WHAT IS AN NFT?

Whether it's digital sports cards or digital artworks, NFTs have taken the internet by storm, with their total amount in USD more than doubling in just the month of February. So, what are these digital properties selling for billions of dollars on anything from niche marketplaces to Christie's, the world's most prestigious auction house?

What does NFT stand for?

An NFT is a blockchain-based non-fungible token. A token is a representation of an asset's ownership. A concert ticket, for example, denotes possession of one concert space.

A Bitcoin is the title of ownership for the Bitcoin's underlying value. On the blockchain, a token is a digital asset. Since the blockchain is transparent, it is simple for everyone to see who owns which token.

A fungible commodity can be readily traded. A dollar is very fungible; you can give it to me in exchange for something and I can re-exchange it for something else. My neighbor lends me a bowl of sugar to bake a nice cake and then buys me another one when he goes to the store in a few days. It makes no difference that the sugar is different; it can be quickly substituted and exchanged.

A non-fungible token is a one-of-a-kind token that cannot be traded for another. The most common use is for artworks. On the blockchain, artworks have been selling for millions of dollars (or in this case a blockchain native currency, Ethereum).

There are many examples, but the most well-known NFT artist is Beeple, who sold 21 pieces of artwork for $3.5 million in the digital marketplace Nifty Gateway. He sold his masterpiece "THE FIRST 5000 DAYS" for $6.5 million at Christie's. Mike Winkelmann, a retired graphic designer from Charleston, South Carolina, is the guy behind Beeple.

In these marketplaces, art isn't the only thing that's traded. Digital sports trading cards are producing a growing amount of volume in the NFT space. Basketball players have now invested more than $230 million exchanging NBA Top Shot cards.

These cards commemorate key moments in the sport's history and only a limited number of each are available. The Ethereum blockchain guarantees the ownership and scarcity of these cards. A rare LeBron James highlight recently sold for a cool $200,000 to the highest bidder.

Why would anyone pay for anything like this?

The most bizarre part of these purchases is that anybody can download Beeple's artwork or LeBron's highlight. It's as simple as pressing the 'save image' button on your laptop.

The evidence of ownership for that artwork, not the artwork itself, is what buyers are after. The buyers are close to art collectors who display their prized possessions in museums. NFTs are a way for art lovers to support their favorite artists financially via the internet.

As humans advance, especially in lockdown, it seems only normal that we will begin to purchase art in the digital world as well. Certain sites, such as Decentraland, go even further, allowing users to purchase land or real estate in the digital world.

Although this has always been a niche aspect of the internet, it has truly burst into mass media in the last six months and seems to be here to stay. Although the first NFT trials took place in 2013-2014, the sector appears to be maturing and gaining mainstream appeal in 2021.

However, there are still a few problems with the NFT market. Transaction fees are very high since Ethereum is the main currency of trade and the network on which marketplaces are established and it is normal to have to pay $50 to move the property title of an NFT from its creator to the buyer.

On platforms like Rarible or OpenSea, the current market leaders, each transaction (creation of the NFT, bids, and transfer of ownership) costs users a lot of money and contributes to the Ethereum network's terrible carbon footprint.

However, there is reason to be optimistic, as Ethereum plans to update its architecture to be even more environmentally friendly by the beginning of 2022. Meanwhile, some marketplaces have devised technological solutions to these constraints.

Drops is a new NFT project that allows you to do a lot more than just buy and sell NFTs. It allows users to build NFTs, bid on them, stake them and borrow money using them as collateral. It also utilizes a Layer 2 approach based on the Polygon network, decreasing transaction costs to a few cents (protected by the platform) while also minimizing major environmental costs.

The most promising aspect of the NFT revolution is that digital artists can be paid for their work for the first time. Because of digital art's essence and its infinite reproducibility, it has been difficult for artists to monetize their work until now. True fans of the artists will now be able to fund them directly without any middlemen or platforms.

The Grammy-winning Kings of Leon released their new album as an NFT, suggesting that mainstream artists have caught on to the trend. Grimes, Lindsay Lohan, and even Soulja Boy, for example, have all released NFTs that reflect music, digital artwork, or even ownership of a limited-edition vinyl.

However, NFTs aren't just for artists; the demand for digital sports cards, for example, has already exploded. So rare, a soccer trading card website, recently sold a one-of-a-kind Kylian Mbappé card for $65,000.

Profiting from at-home sports fans has proven to be immensely lucrative for these sites, attracting the attention of gaming giant Ubisoft, which has now partnered with Sorare for potential ventures.

NFTs are the hottest thing in the recent crypto craze and as more mainstream artists become aware of them, they will only rise in popularity, with a digital market near you soon to follow.

CHAPTER 2

THE HISTORY OF NFT

A non-fungible token is nothing more than a one-of-a-kind digital asset. Bitcoins are fungible, which means that they are all the same and can be used interchangeably. A work of art is an example of a non-fungible token. I can have two similar pieces of digital art, but each one is completely different.

Two NFTs from crypto-artist Josie are seen in the example below. While her two parts, "Choose" edition #4 and "Choose" edition #5, appear to be identical, they are both unique to the blockchain.

Colored coins may be claimed to be the first NFTs ever produced. Colored Coins are small bitcoin denominations, often as small as a single satoshi, the smallest bitcoin unit. Colored coins can be used to display various properties and have various applications, including:

- Real estate

- Vouchers

- Possibility of creating your cryptocurrency

- Shares in a business are given.

- Subscriptions are available.

- Tokens of access

- Collectibles on the internet

Colored Coins represented a significant advancement in Bitcoin's capabilities but their drawback was that they could only represent specific values if everyone agreed on their meaning. Colored Coins were only as strong as their weakest participant since Bitcoin's scripting language was never intended to allow this form of activity inside its network.

Three individuals, for instance, agree that 100 colored coins equal 100 company shares. The entire scheme collapses if even one participant decides that Colored Coins no longer reflect company shares.

Colored coins were first mentioned in a blog post by Yoni Assia in early 2012, titled "bitcoin 2.X— initial specs." he mentions Colored Coins in his post but not concerning them representing different properties or use cases. Instead, he argues that Colored Coins are distinct and recognizable from standard bitcoin transactions because they were part of the "Genesis transaction."

These new assets' potential did not appear to be explored until 4th December 2012, when Rosenfeld Meni published a paper titled "Colored Coins Overview." A few months later, in 2013, another paper titled "Colored Coins — BitcoinX" was published, with authors you may recognize: Vitalik Buterin, Yoni Assia, Lior Hakim, and others.

The shortcomings in Colored Coins are obvious; the system performed best in a permissioned setting, which means that it's easier to use a database in certain situations. Colored Coins, on the other hand, allowed for further innovation and laid the groundwork for NFTs.

The tremendous potential of placing physical assets on distributed ledgers was apparent but implementation needed a more malleable blockchain.

2014 is the year of the Counterparty

Many people realized the massive potential for issuing assets into blockchains after the development of Colored Coins. People also realized that Bitcoin, in its current form, was not designed to support these additional features.

Counterparty, an open-source Internet protocol built on top of the Bitcoin blockchain, was created in 2014 by Dermody Robert, Krellenstein Adam, and Evan Wagner. Counterparty allowed asset development and even had a crypto token with the ticker XCP. It had a trading card game and meme trading among its many projects and properties.

Spells of Genesis on Counterparty, April 2015

Spells of Genesis' creators were among the first to issue in-game assets on a blockchain via Counterparty and launch an ICO. ICOs were initially referred to as "crowdfunding" because they were released too early. Spells of Genesis raised funds for production by releasing BitCrystals, a cryptocurrency that served as the in-game currency.

More Playing Cards on Counterparty in August 2016

Counterparty collaborated with the famous trading card game Force of Will to launch their cards on the platform in Aug. 2016. In North America, Force of Will was the fourth best-selling card game, behind only Pokemon, Yu-Gi-Oh, and Magic:

The Gathering. Since Force of Will was a large mainstream organization with no previous blockchain or cryptocurrency experience, this event was important. Their entry into the ecosystem illustrated the importance of putting such assets on a blockchain.

Rare Pepes on Counterparty, October 2016

Memes were just a matter of time before they made their way to the blockchain. People started issuing "rare pepes" as properties on the Counterparty network in October of 2016. This frog character is featured in a rare Pepe, which is a form of a meme.

These memes have a broad following. There's also a meme exchange known as Rare Pepe. The Uncommon Pepe Meme Directory has experts who certify the Pepe memes' rarity by putting aside the oddness. This example demonstrates that people want exclusive digital objects.

Counterparty now has a slew of projects running on its website, many of which include NFT-like properties. On Counterparty, you can look at the different projects.

Rare Pepes on Ethereum, March 2017

With the emergence of Ethereum in early 2017, memes began to be traded there as well. Peperium was announced in March 2017 as a "and trading card game (TCG) and decentralized marketplace that allowed everyone to build memes that live forever on Ethereum and IPFS," similar to Counterparty.

Peperium had an associated token, Uncommon, which was also used for meme development and paying listing fees, similar to Counterparty.

Cryptopunks, June 2017

As the trading of rare pepes on Ethereum became more popular, two "creative technologists" decided to launch their own NFT project. John Watkinson and Matt Hall discovered they could use the Ethereum blockchain to produce unique characters.

The number of characters would be limited to 10,000 and no two would be identical. Their project was dubbed Cryptopunks in honor of the Cypherpunks who experimented with Bitcoin precursors in the 1990s.

Surprisingly, Watkinson and Hall decided to give a Cryptopunk away for free to anyone with an Ethereum wallet. All 10,000 Cryptopunks were quickly claimed and a flourishing secondary market for buying and selling them arose.

Cryptopunks, interestingly, did not adopt the ERC721 standard because it had not yet been invented but they were also not entirely ERC20 because of its limitations. As a result, Cryptopunks are best represented as a cross between ERC721 and ERC20.

What is the Ethereum Token Standard and how does it work? (ERC)

The Ethereum blockchain has various technical standards for different types of tokens on its network to allow its interactions to function properly. The term "ERC" stands for "Ethereum Request for Comment."

The most widely used standard is ERC20, which contains rules that enable tokens to communicate in predictable ways. When it comes to developing tokens that need to communicate with other tokens or applications on Ethereum, this standard framework is extremely useful.

ERC20 tokens are useful for various functions on Ethereum but they aren't ideal for generating unique tokens. ERC721 was created specifically for this purpose. Although the ERC721 is similar to the ERC20 in many respects, it was developed explicitly to be the technical standard for non-fungible tokens on the Ethereum blockchain.

The key distinction between the two standards is that ERC721 keeps track of individual tokens' ownership and movements in the block, allowing the chain to identify non-fungible tokens. CryptoKitties was the first project to use the new NFT technical standard.

CryptoKitties — October 2017

NFTs have become mainstream thanks to CryptoKitties. Players can adopt, train and exchange virtual cats in CryptoKitties, a blockchain-based virtual game. From CoinDesk to CNN, this incredible project was featured on almost every news outlet. Maybe it was because the game was slowing down and clogging up the Ethereum blockchain. After all, people were making insane amounts of money selling them.

Axiom Zen, a Vancouver-based company, ingeniously released CryptoKitties in October 2017. The team worked on the project for a few months when the alpha version was released during the ETH Waterloo Hackathon, the world's largest hackathon dedicated to the Ethereum ecosystem.

It was the ideal location and time to unveil the game, with over 400 developers in attendance. The team behind CryptoKitties took first place in the hackathon and the game quickly became famous.

CryptoKitties' meteoric rise coincided with the 2017 crypto bull market, adding fuel to the boom. People were going nuts buying, breeding, and selling virtual pets. Many people's eyes were opened to the possibility of non-fungible tokens as a result of this.

Axiom Zen then spun off a Dapper Lab company, which raised $15 million from top investors such as a16z and Google Ventures. People started to understand the true power of NFTs after seeing the operation inside the CryptoKitties group and seeing top investors pour money into Dapper Labs.

NFT Cambrian Explosion 2018–2019

The NFT ecosystem has seen massive growth in 2018 and 2019. There are now over a hundred projects in space, with more in the works. NFT marketplaces are booming, with OpenSea leading the way and SuperRare gaining traction. While the trade volumes are small compared to other crypto markets, they are rapidly increasing and have come a long way.

As Web3 wallets, such as Metamask, develop, integrating into the NFT ecosystem has become easier. Dapper Labs have recently released a Dapper wallet that does not require gas payments. Nftcryptonews AND Nonfungible.com (shameless plug) are two new websites that delve into gameplay guides, NFT market metrics, and general knowledge about space. The current ecosystem is depicted well in this graphic from The Block.

CryptoKitties blazed the NFT trail but they couldn't have done it without the efforts of previous ventures that built unique digital assets to lay the groundwork. The importance of CryptoKitties to the existing NFT ecosystem is shown in a fascinating graphic published by nonfungible.com.

This graph shows that people who own CryptoKitties are more likely to play NFT games, while people who play NFT games are less likely to do so. CryptoKitties serves as an excellent introduction to the world of NFTs.

CryptoKitties may have grown rapidly due to the ability to breed various cats, resulting in creating an entirely ERC721 OR new cat token. Character names, virtual property plots, virtual clothes, event entrance tickets, asteroid mining tools, and other features are now available for NFTs.

The various NFT games and projects collaborating to make things interoperable are perhaps the most exciting development in space. For instance, a player in one game can have a sword transferred to another game and used as a rare clothing piece. The possibilities of interoperability are truly limitless.

What's Next?

Non-fungibles have a much longer history than most people know. The first attempts at NFTs were made during the Colored Coin period in 2012–2013 but I believe we were still early in 2019. Despite the tremendous growth we've seen in the last two years, the industry is still very young and growth will only continue.

In reality, I believe that the NFT ecosystem will continue to expand as more people and businesses recognize the value of NFTs and begin to adopt them. Developers will continue to come up with new applications and interoperable products will be a game-changer. I expect the NFT space to look drastically different in five years than it does now.

CHAPTER 3

WHAT IS DIGITAL ART AND WHAT A DIGITAL CREATOR DOES?

NFTs have become an inevitable subject for someone who makes a living as a creative individual online, sparking a rush to grasp a term that is engulfed in cryptocurrency and blockchain jargon. NFTs, according to others, are part of a digital movement that will democratize fame and allow developers more influence over their fates.

Others worry about the effect of cryptocurrencies on the world and the unrealistic expectations generated by recent reports that digital artist Beeple sold a JPG of his works for $69 million at a Christie's auction.

However, as the movement is reshaping what is considered "valuable" digital art, it is also resurrecting some of the same issues that have troubled artists for centuries: perplexing hype, the whims of affluent collectors, and fraud.

If newcomers want to join the fray before the current wave of interest fades, they must solve practical, logistical, and ethical problems and as some artists transform their digital creations into lucrative products for a new audience of friendly, enthusiastic customers, a question lingers in the background

After speaking with Foundation some months ago, Ellie Pritts, a photographer, and animator from Los Angeles, heard about NFTs. Another artist approached her about the site's digital print market but she later spoke with Foundation's founder, Kayvon Tehranian, who discussed the site's NFT sales.

"I was like, 'I'm not sure what's going on here.' "However, it seems to be very intriguing," she notes. "And there wasn't much detail about it, but it piqued my curiosity. He was the one who taught me about it."

Non-fungible tokens are one-of-a-kind pieces of data that are part of a blockchain that can be purchased and sold using the blockchain's currency. The ones you've been reading about are almost all Ethereum-based.

You've already heard of Bitcoin if you haven't heard of Ethereum. The concept is the same, but the blockchain is different. Although Bitcoin is primarily used to exchange currency, Ethereum is best suited to the exchange of properties.

In principle, any blockchain could support NFTs but this one was designed specifically for them. NFTs can be bought and sold in various online marketplaces, where users can "mine," or make one for any digital purpose.

An NFT does not imply that you own the work of art. Instead, you're simply purchasing metadata that gives a bragging right and the freedom to resell the NFT for a higher price later.

"The people who purchased my pieces did many tests before they bought them. They agreed to invest in me after conducting research and concluding that I was promising." It's a lot to take in and it sounds odd.

Pritts was cynical until February when she minted and sold her first NFT Animation time-consuming and costly to make. It has traditionally been difficult to sell for an affordable price on the internet. She reasoned that NFTs could allow her to do so. Sale, on the other hand, was always pleasurable.

"It's awesome to feel like something I made only because I like it has value," she says. "The people who purchased my pieces did many tests before they bought them. They weren't people I was familiar with. They agreed to invest in me after conducting research and concluding that I was promising."

Buyers aren't embracing creators as "cash grabs instead, she sees NFTs as a new way for writers to reach out to their audiences. Purchasing an artist's work early on gives you a feeling of ownership, similar to seeing a now-famous band perform at their first show. "

Pritts now feels like she's part of a group: she's collaborating on a half-dozen collaborations with other NFT-mining artists she'd never met before joining a month ago. In principle, she claims to have doubled her monthly salary. She hasn't cashed out yet because the money is all in Ether rather than dollars.

"You have to put in the effort."

The jargon barrier is one of the most challenging aspects of understanding NFTs; all of the words used to describe how they work are only familiar to those already familiar with cryptography.

As a result, much of the knowledge about NFTs comes from its most enthusiastic supporters: the marketplaces that sell them, the investors who back them, and the artists who build them. To the rest of the world, it's a problem. However, many artists have turned into guides for others amid the explosion of interest in this new avenue for their work.

Over the past few months, Pinguino Kolb, an artist, and longtime cryptocurrency supporter has been inundated with questions about NFTs from other musicians. "I get many inquiries about why people are so enthusiastic about it. "I've heard it from a couple of my programmer friends who are familiar with crypto space," she says. "They're baffled as to why people are buying it."

Artists have found it more difficult to create their finest work due to monopolistic technology firms' growth. According to William Deresiewicz in this extract from his book "The Death of the Artist," the fundamental problems go far beyond art but they can be solved with bold action.

Her simple response is that it's enjoyable. "I believe it helped to break up the monotony of the pandemic. We're not going to any parties or anything like that. "We aren't going to any art shows," she declares. "Last month, my whole Twitter account was packed with artwork, which was not the case before."

In mid-March, Kolb held a Zoom seminar where she explained everything to artists who had never bought cryptocurrency before. She hopes that knowledge will help people determine whether or not getting involved is a good idea for them. However, this will not be the case for all.

"I don't think that asking an already busy artist to drop everything and get on this train because they're going to miss out is something they can do," she says.

"You can't just make an NFT expect someone to buy it," she says. "You must publicize it. You must put in the requisite effort. You know, you have to be more involved with the culture much of the time. Much of this needs time and if that isn't your main audience, it's probably not something you can do."

"It was immediately morally indefensible."

Kimberly Parker, a Canadian design artist, first heard about NFTs a few years ago when one of the artists she follows started to sell his work.

"I checked in on some of the top artists and was pretty surprised by the amount of money they were earning from these sales," she says, "because much of it was just 2D pictures, JPGs, the kind of work that many of my peers and I were selling for pennies by contrast, if at all."

Even more perplexing was that the art was of varying quality: bad meme art was sold alongside stunning, time-consuming animations, which the same investor often bought.

People purchase NFTs for various reasons, one of which is that they believe they will resell them for a higher profit later. However, this did not deter her from studying NFTs; rather, as she continued her studies, she became increasingly concerned about their environmental effects.

There are a few different ways that blockchains can extend. Ethereum, like Bitcoin, employs the "proof of work" process, in which computers must solve complicated math problems to add new information to the blockchain.

This necessitates computing power, which is scarce and expensive and one factor that adds to the value of cryptocurrencies. It's also why minting an NFT costs money up front, known as a "gas tax."

This processing capacity necessitates the use of electricity, which produces greenhouse gases. Ethereum's pollution production rises in tandem with its development. Bitcoin has a carbon footprint comparable to Switzerland, while Ethereum's is comparable to Tanzania, according to the website Digiconomist's energy consumption tracker.

"It became morally indefensible for someone like me, who is fortunate and willing to support myself already," Parker says.

Anna Podedworna is conscious of NFTs' environmental effects, which is why she is reluctant to start minting them. She, on the other hand, has another reason to think about them.

Podedworna is a Pole who is concerned about Poland's increasingly right-wing, nationalist government. "Having some cryptocurrency-based alternative income sounds better and better," she says. "I mean, I see what's going on in my country and I have a family to think about."

Ethereum has long vowed to turn to an energy-efficient scheme known as proof of stake but in the meantime, some creators purchase carbon offsets to offset the NFTs minted. A filmmaker and animator, Ellie Pritts thinks it is unfair to single out artists for contributing to emissions because there are so many other things that do as well.

Even Ethereum's plans to reduce its carbon footprint, according to Andres Guadamuz, a senior lecturer in intellectual-property law at the University of Sussex who studies cryptocurrencies and copyright, can intensify the inequality that already exists between wealthy early Ethereum investors and everyone else.

Proof of stake replaces the mining process with one that essentially binds mining power to your financial stake in the cryptocurrency, removing the need for massive computing power. "It reinforces the existing inequity," Guadamuz says. "As a result, the people who make all the decisions are already very wealthy in the system."

"That's a lot of money to put on the line."

While it may appear as if NFTs have suddenly become popular, the trend has been building for many years. Cryptokitties, a blockchain game based on Ethereum in which players buy and sell digital cats, debuted in 2017 and rapidly became so popular that it slowed down the entire network's transactions.

Cryptokitties, on the other hand, did not produce nearly the same level of interest as NFTs do now. Essentially, NFTs, according to Guadamuz, have developed in tandem with the ever-increasing buzz surrounding cryptocurrencies in general: an attention economy inside an attention economy.

"You will never be able to match people who started this 10 years ago, no matter how much money you put in right now." But now NFTs are in the news because Ethereum is in the news. After all, is Bitcoin in the news because of the pandemic or low-interest rates?

What are Elon Musk's tweets about?

Whatever the case may be, Guadamuz believes it is crucial to acknowledge the connection between the two. He believes that although artists profit from NFT sales, Ethereum stakeholders benefit even more.

"No matter how much money you put in now, there will always be people who started this ten years ago who you will never be able to match," he says. All of the newcomers are merely earning a portion of a large amount of cryptocurrency that these individuals have amassed over time.

CHAPTER 4

WHAT CRYPTOART IS AND THE FUTURE OF DIGITAL ART

Cryptoart refers to the process of creating a permanent and exclusive digital signature on a digital file of an artwork (tokenizing) and then transferring it to a virtual block to preserve the artwork's scarcity.

As the token holder, you have the option of keeping, selling, or gifting your artworks to other potential buyers, but the original file of your artwork remains yours, safely helmed within your block.

Cryptoart can address issues in the digital art environment by using this newly developed technology: by using blockchain, artists can ensure the scarcity of the artwork they tokenize, preventing art theft and forgeries; the technology can also allow faster and more secure transactions between clients and creators.

The world's understanding of visual art is evolving. It's no wonder that as the world becomes more digital, the way we make, consume, and collect art has changed as well.

The emergence of rare digital art, also known as cryptoart, which combines technology and art to create a new market and medium, has exemplified this paradigm shift in the art world.

The unusual digital art market has sold over $7 million in sales since its launch in 2017 (give or take), with explosive growth in recent months. This movement has spawned online galleries and marketplaces, such as our MakersPlace, that use blockchain technology to secure, authenticate and apply scarcity to digital artworks, which was previously impossible.

Art's Progress

Since the beginning of time, human beings have valued beauty and visual stimulation. Indeed, paleoanthropologists claim that our aesthetic instincts were a core characteristic of humanism in our forefathers, dating back well before the homo sapiens species we now belong to.

For millennia, our universal culture has been characterized by a love of beauty, also known as art. In all of its forms, art has inspired and represented religion, politics, and much more in culture. Across cultures, many scholars attribute the roots of art collecting to religion.

Visual art commissions were most often undertaken by religious figures and organizations in the (relatively) early days of human civilization, with "art collections" mostly housed in places of worship. Visual arts gradually spread through all facets of human culture, giving rise to the "art patron," who gathered purely for the love of art (or the hope of later profit).

The vast majority of the world's population now engages in some kind of art patronage, whether it's personal collecting or viewing the collections of various art institutions worldwide. The world we live in today is nothing like it was a few decades ago. Technology has a tremendous influence on every aspect of our lives.

It would be illogical to leave art out of this evolution. Our ever-evolving encounters with art have culminated in a paradigm shift that has ushered in the next phase of art consumption: the rare digital art revolution, which brings with it a slew of new possibilities for artists and art lovers.

CHAPTER 5
PRINCIPLES AND TERMINOLOGY OF CRYPTOART

We assume that one of the internet's most valuable industries will be fuelled by boundary-pushing and verifiably scarce digital works over the next decade. Cryptoart is a natural progression from the age-old question, "What is art?"

On the other hand, art takes on a more expansive role in a natively interactive medium, intersecting with decentralized finance, virtual worlds, and social experience.

To grasp the potential of cryptoart, it's necessary to place it in the sense of previous art movements. Legacy art movements can be seen as responses to (1) previous art movements, and (2) related cultural phenomena across history.

In the mid-nineteenth century, if you asked "what is art," you would answer realism: the more accurate and practical the art, the better. However, this movement evolved into impressionism.

Artists responded to accuracy by experimenting with conceptual concepts and expressionism and abstract expressionism. Artists manipulated their work for effect, concentrating more on emotional intensity than a literal depiction. (Please note that we are condensing 20,000 Ph.D. dissertations into sixty terms and we recognize that art history is much more complex and nuanced.)

The type of art piece may also be ephemeral and intangible, depending on the cultural context and the artist's viewpoint of street art or performance art.

Although it's impossible to pinpoint an art movement's period while it's occurring, we do know that in modern history, technological developments have had a greater impact on artistic speech.

The artistic work we create and share with the world has become increasingly digitized as our lives have become increasingly digitized. Although "digital" art has been around for nearly four decades, many artists have not reaped the same financial rewards as those who create physical works.

One of the reasons is that most monetization capacity around artistic expression has been predicated on the physical scarcity that moves with art throughout history. A one-time live performance artwork cannot be purchased and resold in the same way Cézanne's The Card Players or Damien Hirst's formaldehyde shark can be purchased and resold for $250 million and $12 million, respectively.

The limitations of temporary art production have also afflicted the digital world. Still, for the opposite reason: the features of a digital original can be perfectly replicated and exchanged. Digital GIFs and MP3s are quickly copied without attribution or reference to the author. There hasn't been a native way to build and monitor digital scarcity that moves with innovative digital property outside legal compliance.

Bitcoin has shown that digital scarcity is possible in the field of money over the last decade. BTC has developed into a commodity money store of value, with a market capitalization of over $100 billion as of this writing.

Ethereum took the idea of digital scarcity beyond commodity currency, allowing any digital good (music, 3D objects files, GIFs, memes) to be made scarce programmatically. These objects are also one-of-a-kind or non-fungible in nature. CoinFund's Jake Brukhman wrote an excellent piece about this concept earlier this week.

ERC 721 is an Ethereum standard interface for non-fungible tokens (i.e., tokens with a unique identifier). We can see any address where it has ever been stored, bid on, or moved, to put it another way, flawless provenance.

We must not confuse an object's reproductive capabilities with its underlying rights regarding blockchain-based art today. The developer of a digital work will imbue it with programmatic scarcity, which is a first step toward demonstrating authenticity.

Property lawyers (including IP lawyers) also think of property rights as a "bundle of rights," similar to how a bundle of sticks is thought of. For a property's lifecycle, all of the different sticks in the package (e.g., use rights, leasing rights, publishing rights, film rights, distribution rights, and so on) may be owned by one person, many people in various combinations.

The first building block for digital artists to begin enjoying property rights and transferring those different rights for their sovereign digital creations is a token's verifiable scarcity over standards like ERC 721. ERC 1155 is based on this concept, allowing owners to establish licenses and model each exclusive right granted by the Copyright Act. Teams like Open Law are expected to continue to innovate in this field.

As a result, cryptoart would be as subversive to conventional art as Bitcoin has been to traditional finance. BTC and cryptoart are more similar than dissimilar, as we'll see below.

Art is a common means of storing value in today's society. Sales of traditional fine art hit $64 billion in 2019 and the overall value of traditional fine art is estimated to be over $3 trillion, but these estimates just scratch the surface.

The wealthiest segment of society powers a significant portion of the existing art market. Still, as cryptoart merges with the markets for collectibles, games, and investments, it promises to introduce a new wave of market investors into art.

Measuring the demand for cryptoart using only data from passengers on private jets is close to measuring the aggregate market for air travel using only data from passengers on private jets.

CHAPTER 6
NFT AND BLOCKCHAIN

In layman's terms, an NFT is a new type of digital collectible object imprinted with a specific bit of code that acts as a permanent record of its validity and is stored on a blockchain. This distributed ledger framework underpins other cryptocurrencies and bitcoin.

These collectibles can be sold and bought like trading cards and since the nature of blockchain technology, a token cannot be counterfeited or removed once it is formed. Artists, artists, and those who want to produce limited-edition digital products can find it useful.

As cryptocurrency enthusiasts and early adopters try to cash in with the trend, the NFT market is exploding. Mike Winkelmann, a South Carolina-based digital artist known as Beeple, recently sold "Everyday: The First 5000 Days," a tokenized compilation of his work for more than $69 million online auctions at Christie's. Other NFTs, such as depicting Homer Simpson as Pepe the Frog, have sold for hundreds of thousands of dollars each.

Since its inception in 2019, NBA Top Shot, the collaboration between the NBA and blockchain startup Dapper Labs that transform basketball highlight videos into one-of-a-kind crypto-collectibles has produced $230 million in revenue. Also, well-known musical acts, such as Kings of Leon, are participating in the NFT by selling millions of dollars' worth of music in the form of digital tokens.

There's no denying that some of the NFT buzzes are inflated. Scammers and get-rich-quick hustlers abound in the cryptocurrency community, with many of their ventures failing. (Do you remember the ICO craze?)

NFTs and other cryptocurrency-related ventures, according to critics, need enormous quantities of energy and processing power, rendering them a growing environmental threat.

There are also legitimate concerns about what NFT buyers are getting for their money. If these tokens become broken links if the marketplaces and hosting services that house the underlying files go away.

However, there is something genuine here that deserves to be taken seriously. Artists, musicians, and other creators have struggled for decades because copying any digital item is trivially simple on the internet.

Since someone who downloaded a file could copy and paste it an infinite amount of times without losing quality, scarcity, the quality that gives offline art its value was difficult to reproduce online.

Blockchain technology changed that by allowing digital goods to be stamped with a cryptographic signature and a permanent record of ownership to be kept.

You can copy the file stored in an NFT as much as you want, but you can't fake the digital signature that protects rare digital goods collectors. NFT supporters believe that in the future, technology could be used to monitor a wide range of items, including property titles, company contracts, and wills.

Creators may also apply a royalty arrangement to their NFTs, entitle them to a portion of the income when their properties are resold. (I tried to make this NFT royalty-free but I couldn't get the Foundation to drop the built-in 10% royalty on secondary sales, so any potential royalties would be donated to the Neediest Cases Fund.

NFTs are quick to ignore, but I'm cautiously positive about them because they represent a new way for creative people to make money online.

Traditional media firms have fought modern, internet-based distribution strategies for years because they saw them as a challenge to their business models, which they were mostly right about. The bulk of what could be found on the internet was free and couldn't be easily copied or pirated.

If you wish to get paid for your work, you have three options: put yourself at the mercy of a licensing service, build a paywall, hire an army of lawyers to enforce your copyright or a large social media network, which, if you were fortunate or exceptionally successful, could share some of its advertising revenue with you.

Digital subscriptions are one way for artists to reclaim the power of their careers. Another possibility is the use of non-fluorescent transistors (NFTs). NFTs could erode social media middlemen's economic supremacy by allowing artists, musicians, and, yes, journalists to transform individual works into one-of-a-kind digital collectible pieces.

CHAPTER 7

NFTS AS COLLECTIBLES AND DIGITAL ASSETS

NFTs are now used in some projects as collectible and tradable objects. Let's take a look at a few of the more well-known ones.

Decentralization

Decentraland is a decentralized virtual reality environment where players can own and trade virtual land and other NFT products in-game. Cryptovoxels is a game that allows players to create, build and trade virtual property.

Gods Unchained

Gods Unchained is a blockchain-based digital collectible card game in which cards are released as NFTs. Since each digital card is one-of-a-kind, players can own and trade them in the same way they can physical cards.

My Favorite Crypto Heroes

My Crypto Heroes is a multiplayer role-playing game (RPG) in which players level up historical heroes by completing quests and fighting in wars. On the Ethereum blockchain, the heroes and in-game objects are issued as tokens.

Binance Collectibles is a set of Binance tokens.

Binance Collectibles are NFTs released by Binance and Enjin in partnership on special occasions. If you want to get your hands on one, follow Binance on Twitter and keep an eye out for our upcoming giveaways! If you'd like to join an NFT giveaway, just follow these simple instructions:

Install an Ethereum-compatible wallet, such as Trust Wallet.

Copy your Ethereum address and enter it into the giveaway according to the rules. You may have to fill out a form or leave a Twitter message. Double-check the rules and make sure you know what you need to do to join.

Stamps in Cryptocurrency

The Austrian Postal Service issues Crypto Stamps, which connect the digital and physical worlds. These stamps, like any other stamp, are used to transport mail. However, they are also saved on the Ethereum blockchain as digital images, making them a tradable digital collectible.

Outside of traditional financial applications, digital collectibles opens blockchain technology to a whole new set of possibilities. NFTs can be a crucial part of the blockchain community, and the broader economy, by representing tangible assets in the digital environment.

The possibilities are infinite and many developers are sure to come up with fresh and exciting applications for this promising technology. According to a 2020 study from software monitoring company L'Atelier BNP Paribas and nonfungible.com, non-fungible tokens or NFTs - items that act as digital assets - have risen to encompass a $250 million industry.

CHAPTER 8

COMMON NFT MARKETPLACE

Non-fungible tokens are FTs. They're one-of-a-kind things that can't be replaced with anything else. A one-of-a-kind trading card, for example, is an NFT since another card cannot replace it.

You get something different if you swap your card for another card. These are distinct from fungible objects, which are often interchangeable. If you exchange one bitcoin for another, for example, you will be in the same place as when you began.

On the other hand, if you exchange a virtually useless mass-produced baseball card from the late 1980s for a 1909 American Tobacco Company T206 Honus Wagner card (worth over $1 million), you've done incredibly well for yourself.

The majority of NFTs are now digital. This makes it especially simple for creators to offer something special and unique to their fans. Some NFTs, for example, are digital artworks, which are now being collected in the same way that collectors have been collecting physical paintings for years and some of these NFTs have fetched astronomical sums. At Christie's, an NFT artwork by Beeple, a digital artist, sold for $69 million.

NFTs are identical to other cryptocurrencies and Bitcoin in many respects, with the difference that they are non-divisible and non-fungible. The first NFTs were part of the Ethereum blockchain, which stores additional electronic data to differentiate them.

NTFS is now supported by other blockchains as well. Since different NFTs use different blockchain technologies, not all NFT marketplaces buy and sell all NFTs. Creators often choose NFT marketplaces based on whether they accept a particular NFC token standard. ERC-721 and ERC-1155 are the two Ethereum specifications that have been published so far.

Binance, a competitor, has since published BEP-721 and BEP-1155 standards. Since they allow many NFTs to be transacted and bunched together, the two "1155" standards vary from the original "721" standards. Most NFT platforms enable customers to have a digital wallet and pay for their transactions with cryptocurrencies.

1. OpenSea

OpenSea boasts of being the world's biggest NFT marketplace. Art, virtual worlds, censorship-resistant domain names, sports, trading cards, and collectibles are among the non-fungible tokens available. ERC721 and ERC1155 properties are included. Unique digital assets such as Axis, ENS titles,

CryptoKitties, Decentraland, and more are available to purchase, sell and discover. They have over 700 projects, ranging from trading card games and collectible games to interactive art projects and name systems such as ENS (Ethereum Name Service).

With OpenSea's item minting tool, creators can build their

blockchain pieces. It allows you to create a set and NFTs without writing a single line of code. You can easily join OpenSea if you're working on a smart contract for a game, a digital collection, or another project involving unique digital objects on the blockchain.

If you're selling something on OpenSea, you have the option of selling it for a set price, a declining price listing, or an auction listing.

2. Rarible

Rarible is a community-owned NFT marketplace that uses the ERC-20 RARI token as its "ownership" token. Rarible rewards active users who purchase or sell on the NFT marketplace with the RARI token. Per week, it distributes 75,000 RARI.

Art assets are given special attention on the website. Rarible allows creators to "mine" new NFTs to sell their works, whether they're books, music albums, digital art, or movies. The developer can also show a sneak preview of their creation to anyone who visits Rarible but only the purchaser will access the entire project.

Rarible is a website that buys and sells NFTs in some categories, including photography, art, games, metaverses, music, domains, memes, and more.

3. SuperRare

SuperRare is primarily a platform for people to sell and buy one-of-a-kind, limited-edition digital artworks. Each piece of art is created by a network artist and tokenized as a crypto-collectible digital object that you can own and trade. They identify themselves as a cross between Instagram and Christie's, providing a new way to engage with art, culture, and collecting on the internet.

Each piece of art on SuperRare is digitally collectible, a digital item that is encrypted and tracked on the blockchain. On top of the marketplace, SuperRare has created a social network. Digital collectibles are suitable for a social setting because they have a simple record of ownership.

The Ethereum network's native cryptocurrency, ether, is used in all transactions. SuperRare only works with a select group of hand-picked artists; Also, you can use a form to apply your artist profile and be considered for their upcoming full launch.

Foundation is a niche forum that brings together digital developers, crypto natives, and enthusiasts to advance culture. It's called the "new creative economy." It is primarily

4. Foundation

Concerned with digital art.

In August 2020, they revealed an open call for developers to experiment with crypto and play with the idea of value in their first blog post on their website. "Hack, subvert and exploit the value of artistic work," they encouraged artists.

When an NFT trades on Base, the artist receives 10% of the secondary transaction value, i.e, when a collector resells their work to someone else for a higher price, the artist receives 10% of the sales value.

5. AtomicMarket

AtomicMarket is an NFT market smart contract with mutual liquidity that is used by many websites. Anything listed on one market appears on all other markets, which is known as shared liquidity.

It's a marketplace for Atomic Properties, a non-fungible token standard built on the eosio blockchain. The Atomic Asset standard can be used to tokenize and build digital assets and purchase, sell and auction assets in the Atomic Assets marketplace.

On the AtomicMarket, you can both list your own NFTs for sale and search for existing listings. NFTs from well-known collections are marked with a verified checkmark, making it easier to identify genuine NFTs. Collections that are malicious are put on a blacklist.

6. The Myth Market

Myth Market is a set of user-friendly online marketplaces that appeal to a range of digital trading card brands. GoPepe. Market, GPK.Market, Heroes. Market, KOGS.Market and Shatner. The market is the featured markets at the moment

7. BakerySwap

BakerySwap is a decentralized exchange (DEX) and Binance Smart Chain automated market maker. It makes use of a BakerySwap token that is native to the platform (BAKE).

BakerySwap is also a multi-functional crypto hub that includes a crypto launchpad and (NFT) a non-fungible token supermarket and some decentralized finance (Defi) services.

Its NFT supermarket sells digital art, meme contests, and NFT games, all of which can be purchased with BAKE tokens. You can win bonus BAKE tokens by using NFTs in 'combo meals.' It's also a simple and clear method to mint and sell your artwork.

8. KnownOrigin

KnownOrigin is an online marketplace where you can find and purchase exclusive digital artwork. Every piece of digital art on KnownOrigin is genuine and one-of-a-kind.

Creators may use the forum to show off their work and sell it to collectors who value authenticity. The Ethereum blockchain protects it. Creators can upload digital artwork to the KnownOrigin gallery as a jpg or Gif file, with all files stored on IPFS.

9. Enjin Marketplace

Enjin Marketplace is a forum for exploring and exchanging blockchain properties. It is the official Enjin-based NFT marketplace. To date, it has allowed the spending of $43.8 million worth of Enjin Coin on digital assets, totaling 2.1 billion NFTs. There have been 832.7K trades. The Enjin Wallet makes it easy to list and buy gaming goods and collectibles.

From game item collections like the Multiverse and games, The Six Dragons, like Age of Rust, gamified reward programs like community-created collectibles, Microsoft's Azure Heroes, and

NFTs by companies like Swissborg and Binance, the Projects page showcases Enjin-powered blockchain projects.

10. Part

A portion is an online marketplace that uses Blockchain technology to link artists and collectors to easily sell, invest in, and own art and collectibles while maintaining total transparency. It involves the Artist Collective, a decentralized global network of artists and creators.

Anyone can be a collector thanks to Part. You can keep track of both your physical and digital collections in one place, making it simple to swap cryptocurrency for art and collectibles.

Portion Tokens are Ethereum Blockchain ERC-20 assets used to decentralize governance and vote on the platform's future. Liquidity mining, artist awards, collaborations, and potential team members all receive new tokens. When artists create new NFTs, they are also given new Portion Tokens, which are currently worth 500 PRT.

Async Art is a type of art that is created in real-time.

Async Art is a blockchain-based artistic movement. Programmable art can be made, collected, and traded. Both "Layers" and "Masters" are available for purchase. While Layers are the individual components that make up the Master image, A Master is a 1/1 edition art piece.

Layers are endowed with unique abilities determined by the artist. When you alter something on a Layer, the Master image will represent this regardless of who owns it.

Artists pick the parameters of their art and give exclusive control over every aspect to individual collectors. For example, they could let someone change the state of the background, the location of a character, or the color of the sky. Since February 2020, the site has seen over $6 million in bid value and over $1.5 million in artist sales.

CHAPTER 9
HOW TO CREATE NFT

I know you'll have questions about whether or not NFTs are worthwhile. Consider, for a moment, the world of traditional art. You see art galleries and people paying hundreds of thousands or millions of dollars for artwork and then reality hits you. Under the right conditions, only a very few will make a living doing it. Even then, they must divide the benefits with other parties involved in the deal.

NFTs live in a special environment. You, the artist, have complete control over all of the strings that make up your work. NFT marketplaces are foreign marketplaces that display your work to the entire world. To sell your work, you don't need to go to a gallery or an agency. You are not forced to share a portion of your earnings with middlemen.

NFT marketplaces, in reality, keep you updated on the selling of your artwork at all times. You can earn a reasonable commission from your artwork's NFT once it is traded.

You may also prove the validity of your work at any time and that there is only one true owner of your artwork at any given time. Overall, the NFT artwork ecosystem makes it easier for anyone to purchase and sell art.

Creating your NFTs requires little or no technological expertise, contrary to popular belief. You can create NFTs for your artwork in minutes using NFT marketplaces like OpenSea, Rarible, or Mintable.

You must first link your crypto wallet to the NFT marketplace of choice before you can begin building your NFT. You'll never have to share any other information because the wallet address would be your login information. After that, go to the marketplace's "Build" area, upload your artwork and complete the process by pressing the necessary buttons.

That is the end of the discussion. You'll get your NFT artwork ready to sell before your mother summons you downstairs for dinner, your baby begins to weep or your better half misses you.

Fungible means that it can be quickly replaced. A 1 of 1 Mickey Mantle rookie card is not just any baseball card, rather it's irreplaceable and non-fungible. Oil is fungible because any barrel is as good as the next.

When non-fungible assets are tokenized, the token becomes a digital representation of the asset's important data. Tokens are stored in wallets, each of which has its address. Token IDs link to wallet addresses on the blockchain, a massive, publicly accessible database that allows anyone to verify digital ownership.

The most common sites for NFT development are OpenSea and Rarible. Although Rarible has the most overall sales, OpenSea offers additional services, such as the ability to build your own NFT website using the OpenSea exchange. Users can upload their artwork and build collections on both platforms without knowing anything about blockchain technology.

Remember that there will be some initial costs before you begin. A blockchain, usually Ethereum's blockchain powers NFTs. To tokenize your art, you'll need to pay a network fee known as gas.

During the development process, Rarible allows artists to mint NFTs on the blockchain (on-chain). As a result, the prices will be lower in the future. Rarible is your best bet if you intend on selling a few NFTs for astronomical prices. You can use OpenSea's Collection Manager, on the other hand, if you want to make a large number of inexpensive NFTs.

Users can create a new set with OpenSea Collection Manager for a one-time fee. The OpenSea centralized team can build and store an infinite amount of NFTs off-chain before a sale is made using that set. Your NFT will be put on the chain and transferred after the buyer pays the transaction's gas tax.

This chapter will guide you through the steps to make your own NFTs in an OpenSea set.

1st Step - Setup MetaMask

Setting up a software wallet is the first step in creating your own NFT. You'll need to use this wallet to store your NFTs and to pay blockchain gas fees.

Go to metamask.io to get the software or install the chrome extension. It is fast and free to create a MetaMask wallet. Only keep hold of your seed phrase in case you need to retrieve the wallet in the future.

Keep in mind that wallets do not store cryptocurrency or NFTs; rather, they store your private key, which is needed to approve transactions. Both cryptocurrencies and NFTs are stored on the blockchain and the wallet ID is used to identify who owns what.

2ND Step - Tokenize your art

You'll be able to make your NFTs once you've set up a MetaMask wallet. Go to opensea.io and pick Build from the menu bar. You can now use OpenSea to link your MetaMask wallet.

Click the Add New Item button after giving your NFT set a name. You can now upload the file you want to tokenize and allocate its properties and statistics to set it apart from the rest of your array.

Establish a retail price after determining how many copies of each item you need.

3rd Step - Make a marketplace listing.

You must first authorize OpenSea to sell products from your account before you can sell your first NFT. You would have to pay a gas tax since this is a blockchain purchase. You're good to go if you send any Ether to your MetaMask. This fee is only needed when you create an NFT collection for the first time.

You can buy Ethereum on Coinbase or Gemini and send it to your MetaMask wallet if you don't already have any. Start with Benzinga's guide to buying Ethereum if you're new to cryptocurrencies. Anyone can find and buy NFTs on the OpenSea marketplace now that you've granted OpenSea permission to sell them. It's over!

There are three key ways to generate NFT gains in the industry: scalping, investing, and trading.

For most people, investing in a platform like Nifty Gateway, OpenSea or Rarible is their best bet for cashing in on the NFT bubble before it bursts. The majority of miners went home empty-handed during the California gold rush, but those who sold picks and shovels made a fortune.

It could be worthwhile for you to build your own NFTs for your fans if you're an artist or influencer. Logan Paul, a YouTuber, and professional boxer made $5 million in one day by selling 3,000 NFTs for one Ether each. NFT FOMO has hit new heights. If you have a knack for forecasting resale demand, pick up a $300 Nifty Gateway bot from Upwork and get scalping!

NFTs also represent real and digital objects. The NBA, for example, is tokenizing clips of the greatest basketball plays in history and selling them for a fortune — and they get a 5% share of all secondary market sales — another advantage of NFTs for makers.

Tokenized pictures of 24 x 24-bit avatars make up the crypto punks. There are 10,000 crypto punks, each one special and selling for an average of $15,000 each.

There are 9 aliens, 24 primates, 88 zombies, 3,840 females, and 6,039 males, each with their characteristics and rarity. Just 44 crypto punks have the "beanie" trait, making them immediately more valuable than one of the 332 crypto punks with VR goggles.

The blockchain is changing the way we think about art and collectibles, but it's just the start. Tokenization is a versatile technique with a multitude of applications yet to be explored.

NFTs seem to have a long life ahead of them. Another issue is which NFTs would be able to withstand the test of time and maintain their value. Each NFT set has its value proposition but in the end, they are only worth what someone is willing to pay for them.

Given enough time, the vast majority of all NFTs produced will become virtually useless. Some, on the other hand, can rise in value and popularity.

CHAPTER 10
HOW TO BUY NFT

Non-fungible tokens are somewhat distinct from other investments in cryptocurrencies. Like other cryptocurrencies, these tokens do not have value based on their usefulness. Instead, the media attached to NFTs gives them meaning — the most popular types of media on NFTs today are art and music, but NFTs can tokenize any real-world asset.

NFTs are Ethereum-based tokens that are used to validate ownership of the asset associated with the token. Although NFTs are costly, you are getting more than a JPEG file. Make an account on the NFT Marketplace in the first phase.

NFTs can be bought and sold on various websites. You'll be able to buy various styles of art or collectibles depending on the marketplace you want.

Some of the most well-known NFT marketplaces are as follows:

Opensea is known as an Ethereum-based market for non-fungible tokens. Users can swap non-fungible tokens for cryptocurrencies through the network. It sells everything from video game pieces to digital artwork.

NFTs have their social network called SuperRare. Each piece on the platform is one-of-a-kind and users can purchase and sell these one-of-a-kind pieces through the platform's website. To make a purchase, you'll need to finance your account with Eth tokens since the platform runs on the Ethereum network.

The famous cryptocurrency exchange Gemini owns Nifty Gateway, an NFT marketplace. Famous artists including Steve Aoki, Grimes, 3LAU, and others collaborate to release artwork in the primary marketplace.

Collectors may resell their artwork on the company's secondary market. You can use Ethereum to finance your Nifty account or you can use the website to add a credit card.

NBA Top Shot is a website where you can buy and sell officially licensed NBA memorabilia. These digital basketball cards are more interactive than traditional trading cards and are a new take on basketball cards. In-game clips of the featured teams, for example, are included on the cards.

A LeBron James Dunk card, which featured a clip of James dunking on the Houston Rockets and sold for more than $200,000, was the most expensive card sold on NBA Top Shot.

Step 1

Sorare is an online store where you can buy and sell limited-edition soccer NFT cards. There are currently over 125 clubs listed, with more being added every week. Connect and trade with other fans in Sorare's open marketplace or play the Global Fantasy Football Game, where you can build your lineup and earn points based on real-life results.

Step 2: Deposit into your bank account.

You can buy Ethereum on a cryptocurrency exchange and send your crypto to your marketplace account if you already have an account with one. eToro and Coinbase are decent choices for beginners if you don't have a crypto exchange account already.

Step 3 - Purchase your NFT

After your account has been funded, buying an NFT is a simple operation. You'll need to make an offer for the NFT you want to buy because most marketplaces are set up as auctions. For NFTs with many prints, some marketplaces function more like an auction, using the highest bid and lowest ask.

The future resale value of an NFT purchased directly from the primary marketplace is a bonus. Some high-demand NFTs will sell for 5 to 10 times their initial price shortly after their release. The disadvantage of purchasing NFTs on the open market is that it is difficult to predict demand. You can equate your purchase to previous purchases in the secondary marketplace.

CHAPTER 11
HOW TO SELL NFT

Digital trading cards, art, virtual real estate, and gaming are all examples of NFTs. NFTs, unlike common cryptocurrencies such as Bitcoin and Ether, cannot be directly traded and are distributed through some platforms. Most NFT platforms demand that customers have a digital wallet and use cryptocurrencies such as Ethereum, WAX, or Flow.

The majority of digital-art trading platforms allow artists to collect royalty. Some art platforms cater to a select group of artists, while others allow everyone to create and sell their work.

NFTs also provided a windfall of benefit for professional digital artists. Last week, Trevor Jones, an NFT artist, told Insider that digital art trading platforms could prevent the need for more traditional art markets.

NFTs have also piqued the interest of many conventional auction houses. Christie's, a 1766-founded auction house, auctioned a Beeple piece in February, marking the company's first foray into the digital token market. With two days left in the auction, the piece is currently valued at $9.75 million.

Platforms like Super Rare, Nifty Gateway Foundation allow buyers to choose from carefully curated work by multimillion-dollar digital artists like Griffin Cock Foster and Beeple. Duncan, co-founders of Nifty Gateway, told Insider that their firm deals with artists one-on-one.

"One of the best things about Nifty Gateway is that there are all these artists who essentially just existed on Instagram or Twitter doing all this very special work but never had a way to make money off it," Griffin Cock told Insider. "They began selling cryptoart and they're still reaping the rewards and gaining popularity."

Names like Grimes and digital comic artist Chris Torres have appeared on Nifty Gateway, Super Rare, and Foundation platforms. Artists will earn up to 10% royalties for all potential sales of their work across these channels.

Although Nifty Gateway aims to make its platform more open to buyers by encouraging them to pay with a credit card, other platforms place a greater emphasis on lowering the entry barrier for developers. Zora and Rarible are invite-only platforms, while Mintable and Rarible allow users to upload and sell images and text as NFTs.

Artists can still receive royalties on these pages but they aren't as well-curated. Rarible allows users to upload everything from blank pictures to their interpretations of well-known works of art. NFTs can be bought for as little as $10 or as much as hundreds of thousands of dollars on these websites.

OpenSea bills itself as the world's largest non-traditional marketplace, with everything from art to virtual reality, sports, and trading cards available. About 200 categories and 4 million products are available on the website.

On OpenSea, either can be used to purchase common NFT products such as CryptoPunks, CryptoKitties, and virtual real estate. OpenSea has been dubbed "the eBay of the blockchain" by DappRadar, a blog that monitors and analyzes decentralized apps.

Decentraland, a popular virtual real-estate website, is one of the marketplaces that runs on OpenSea. According to DappRadar, OpenSea sold nearly $24 million worth of NFTs last week.

NFT revenues are strongly affected by sports.

NBA Top Shot has a wide variety of sports clips for sale, ranging from $20 to thousands of dollars. NBA Top Shot has a wide range of sports clips for sale, ranging from $20 to thousands of dollars. Top Shots in the NBA

According to CryptoSlam, NBA Top Shot, a website where people can purchase video highlights as NFTs, has sold over $260 million worth of NFTs in the last month. In February, a LeBron James dunk set the record for the most expensive Top Shot, selling for $208,000 in Flow.

Fantasy sports have impacted NFT revenues. So rare is a fantasy soccer game that allows users to purchase, sell and manage virtual teams using digital player cards. According to CryptoSlam, one of the top ten most popular crypto-collectible platforms is Axie Infinity, which sells cartoon characters designed to battle, similar to Pokmon.

According to CoinDesk, in 2020, the site had over 10,000 monthly active users, making it Ethereum's most popular game. Looking Glass Factory, a platform that produces digital holograms and sells them as tokens, is one of the many sites that have found success in the niche NFT collectible sector.

CHAPTER 12

HOW TO INVEST IN NFT AND HOW NFTS CAN BE AN ADDITION TO CRYPTO ASSET PORTFOLIOS

The idea of NFTs or non-flammable tokens that represent a digital artwork or other digitally collectible item is the newest investment craze. "Fungible" is a concept that defines something that can be easily substituted for something of similar value.

A non-fungible object is a one-of-a-kind item that cannot be replaced. NFTs allow anyone to buy or sell a one-of-a-kind work of digital art, with the buyer being the sole owner. Although NFTs are a new type of investment, some have already sold for millions of dollars, illustrating their value, but, are they the right investment for you?

NFTs are blockchain-based tokens that contain details about a single digital work of art. There are almost no limits to the types of art that can be bought as NFTs. Twitter's CEO, Jack Dorsey, made headlines recently when he sold the first tweet as an NFT for $2.9 million. Nyan Cat, a ten-year-old meme, was the star of a $500-thousand-dollar animated GIF. A digital painting by Beeple, a digital artist, was sold for $69 million.

Similar to physical fine art sales, buying art isn't what brings in the big bucks; it's selling art to the highest bidder. Like physical art, you can buy a Mona Lisa print, but there will only ever be one original Mona Lisa.

Since NFTs are such a recent investment, there is still a lot to learn about them. Furthermore, valuing digital art can be difficult, making NFTs a high-risk investment. When you invest in stocks, the stock price decides how much your investment is worth. Buying a stock at a low price and then selling it at a higher price can be profitable.

The worth of digital art, on the other hand, is measured by how much someone is willing to pay for it. Since there are no set guidelines for assessing the worth of a meme, GIF, or tweet, it's anyone's guess how much you'll be able to get for it — whether you can sell it at all.

A set of gold coins

If you're serious about investing in NFTs, set a budget and just buy what you can afford to lose. Since NFTs are so speculative, don't expect to make any money from them. Investing the rest of the money in safer investments like index funds or exchange-traded funds is also a good idea (ETFs).

NFTs are a modern type of investment but they aren't for everybody. It's not a bad idea to get your feet wet if you're interested in NFTs and have some cash to spare. Otherwise, it's preferable to stay on the sidelines and watch this phenomenon unfold from a safe distance.

Mega-cap companies like Sotheby's and Christie's, and online companies like eBay and Etsy, now help us sell and benefit from our collections. To cover themselves from fraud and injuries, people spend a small fortune on insurance. Many who are well-informed will amass significant capital.

NFTs are treated in the same way. Many people will want to own the original, even though digital artwork is easier to copy and distribute. A mixture of love and pride inspires many people; Brunei's Sultan is said to own 7,000 vehicles.

On the other hand, others wish to express their gratitude to the original artist for creating something they want. On Etsy, tens of thousands of independent digital artists sell their work for under $100 and if you like a specific artist, I strongly advise you to buy a cheap piece or two, even if it's just to keep the creators doing what they're doing.

Investors must have a unique understanding of the assets represented by NFTs to profit from them. Basketball fans who can correctly forecast future NBA superstars can buy low-cost highlight reels now and profit millions when the stars break out in a few years. Both Steve Nash and Kobe Bryant had disappointing rookie seasons (Kobe scored 7.6 points per game at 18!)

Both, on the other hand, would go on to become superstars in the future. Any team that bet on them early would have made any money. Those who buy NBA one-hit wonders as NFTs during their 15 minutes of fame, on the other hand, are unlikely to succeed.

Similarly, in the art world, there have always been duds and stars. Most early works of Banksy were painted over by officials who mistook them for graffiti. Meanwhile, his later works will sell for as much as Rembrandt's at auction, ordinary people have trouble telling the difference between masterpieces and standard works of art.

To put it another way, focus on your area of specialization if you want to make any money in NFTs. Check out Decentraland, a virtual world operated by Ethereum, if you enjoy video games (CCC: ETH-USD). If you're a sports fan with a keen eye for talent, the NBA's NFTs may be for you. Make art or music your area of expertise if you're talented in those fields.

Investing in NFTs requires two leaps of confidence. The first is self-evident: the underlying asset must be valuable and growing to be profitable. If you think the artist can make an infinite number of copies of a digital art piece, it's pointless to purchase it.

The second leap of confidence is a little more difficult: NFT buyers must trust the entire cryptocurrency framework. You are issued a token when you buy an NFT that marks you as a specific asset owner.

This is done often on the Ethereum network, which runs the Ether cryptocurrency. Cardano (CCC: ADA-USD) and Polkadot (CCC: DOT1-USD) are two new coins that have recently entered the fray.

So, what can you do to boost your chances?

When purchasing an NFT, you must ensure that the property is not owned by someone else. In the real world, title insurance is a multibillion-dollar industry that guarantees you don't purchase a property where the seller has lied about ownership. However, if you want to stop receiving a tampered with or copyrighted object, you must do your homework in the world of NFTs.

As a result, investors should avoid putting too much money into any one NFT. Even if you expect an asset to double or quadruple in value, you can limit your gross investible portfolio to 5% to 10% of your total investible portfolio to cover yourself if something goes wrong. In the worst-case scenario, all the best assets would be rendered worthless.

Simultaneously, don't overextend yourself. If you buy a thousand pieces of low-quality digital art, a 10x champion will not move the needle.

CHAPTER 13
UNDERSTANDING NFT STOCKS

When you consider the art's resale value, NFTs become a compelling investment opportunity. It's close to purchasing physical works of art. If you just want to keep the art, having possession of it will not benefit you.

Of course, staring at the work of art can provide you with a sense of fulfillment. Big money, though, comes from selling pieces of art to the highest bidder. To put it another way, if you can buy a one-of-a-kind NFT and then sell it for more than you paid for it, you will benefit handsomely.

The strength of blockchain is that it eliminates the possibility of fraud and theft. There will be codes and authentication to confirm and validate the authenticity of the work of art you own. Others can also create copies of an original digital art piece but only one original remains. The original belongs to the person who owns the NFT for that art piece.

If anyone asked you in January what NFT stocks were, you'd probably stare at them blankly. The enthusiasm has sparked Wall Street rallies in a slew of tech stocks this week. As I previously said, some of these have little to do with the NFT niche. However, based on speculation, investors believe these companies will gain exposure to NFTs.

It's difficult to tell if NFT stocks will take off in the long run at this stage. Examine cannabis stocks and cryptocurrencies from 2017 to 2019. If history is any guide, the excitement surrounding NFT stocks will likely fade away soon.

With all of the hype, it's easy to dismiss it as science fiction that will never come to pass. However, if we look closely, we can see that something is going on behind the scenes and why am I saying this?

Last year, according to Nonfungible.com, the overall volume of NFT transactions increased to $250 million. NFT transactions totaled more than $220 million last month alone. It seems that we are experiencing something that is rising at an unprecedented rate.

Traditionally, any digital art that is shared, saved, or downloaded on the internet can be easily shared, saved, and downloaded. However, since anybody can use it, there isn't a clear sense of ownership. Assume you're an artist, a particularly talented one.

You also produce some of the most stunning works of art, but what about putting your imagination to good use?

You seem to have had little success with it so far, at least with most citizens. However, there is a way to give digital art a sense of individuality using NFTs. It also provides an opportunity for good artists to continue doing innovative works.

The art industry has many scopes for NFTs. However, first and foremost, the market must be regulated. There is currently no law dictating who is allowed to build NFTs and who is not. Before then, I wouldn't invest in NFT stocks without first waiting for the dust to settle but, don't get me wrong: I love art.

I genuinely believe that this has the potential to change the way art is perceived in our culture. Maybe it's just me, but before investing in NFT stocks, I'd like to see more concrete developments. However, this is merely my opinion; the final decision is yours to make. Make sure you do your homework and study.

The hunt for stocks linked to non-fungible tokens (is heating up and then investors are frantically looking for opportunities. The fact that crypto-assets are starting to stir up mainstream knowledge is behind the interest in NFT stocks. Celebrities such as Jack Dorsey and Elon Musk have experimented with offerings and brands are following suit.

Are you the sort of investor who is willing to take on a high level of risk in exchange for the possibility of a high return?

NFT stocks can be erratic. As you'll see below, many businesses are experimenting with NFT offerings. Others use a mix of online sleuthing and social media gossip to reach new heights. As a result, the early-stage trend is extremely hot but also extremely risky.

When evaluating these businesses, make sure to weigh the risks and do your research into what makes them special.

Do you think it's great that they're associated with NFT targets or blockchain technology?

Are their companies ripe for potential cryptocurrency deals?

Do they have any NFT services that produce revenue?

There is money to be made in the room as digital artist Beeple made nearly $70 million for a single piece, but there is also money to be lost.

With that in mind, here are the top ten NFT stocks that InvestorPlace is currently tracking.

- Takung Art is a form of martial art (NYSEMKT: TKAT)

- Jiayin Group is a Chinese conglomerate (NASDAQ: JFIN)

- Group of Oriental Culture (NASDAQ: OCG)

- Media in Liquid Form (NASDAQ: YVR)

- Hall of Fame Resort & Entertainment is a resort and entertainment complex located in Las Vegas, Nevada (NASDAQ: HOFV)

- Funko Pop! (NASDAQ: FNKO)

- Cinedigm is a film production company that specializes in (NASDAQ: CIDM)

- Color Star Technology is a technology that allows you to see colors (NASDAQ: CSCW)

- WiseKey is a program that allows you to create a (NASDAQ: WKEY)

- KBS Fashion Group is a fashion company based in Korea (NASDAQ: KBSF)

CHAPTER 14

NFTS FOR GAMING, DIGITAL IDENTITY, LICENSING, CERTIFICATES, AND FINE ART

Collectibles, art, games, and virtual worlds are the key categories of existing NFT use cases. Other categories, such as sports, fashion, and real-world properties, are, however, increasingly growing.

Terra Virtua is one of the world's first immersive digital collectible networks, with some of Hollywood's biggest names, including Topgun, The Godfather series, Pacific Rim, Sunset Boulevard Lost in Space, among others. It also has a relationship with Paramount Pictures.

1. Antiques and collectibles

Collectibles are currently one of the most common applications of NFTs in terms of sales volume, accounting for about 23.6 percent of all sales in the previous month. CryptoPunks, which debuted in June 2017 and has since sold for thousands of dollars, is one of the first collectible NFTs on Ethereum.

They were created before ERC-721 was launched and a wrapper had to be created for them to be traded on exchanges such as Opensea. CryptoKitties have become well-known collectibles, with sales reaching more than $38 million since their launch in November 2017,

2. Playing video games

Gamers, as previously said, are an ideal target market for NFTs since they are already acquainted with virtual worlds and currencies. The gaming industry is booming thanks to NFTs, which enable in-game objects to be tokenized and easily transferred or traded using peer-to-peer trading and marketplaces.

On the other hand, traditional games forbid the selling or transferring in-game objects such as uncommon weapons and skins.

Since players have full control of their digital properties, NFTs make the gaming experience more tangible and satisfying. They're also spawning a new economy, as players can now benefit from their in-game properties by constructing and improving them.

3. Artpiece

One of the most challenging problems for digital artists is copyright infringement, but NFTs are a remedy because they provide evidence of ownership, authenticity and eliminate counterfeiting and fraud concerns.

As museums and galleries close due to COVID-19, many artists have switched to NFTs and online showrooms, according to a Coindesk post, and "just as Bitcoin paved the way for peer-to-peer transactions by establishing a public events ledger, cryptoart has provenance built-in."

In July, "Picasso's Bull" set a new record for the NFT highest-valued art auction sale, selling for more than $55,000. "These ventures can also boost and streamline artists' income by linking them directly to customers via blockchain-based payment and exchange solutions," according to Cointelegraph.

4. Interactive universes

Digital worlds are another application for NFTs. Users can build, own and monetize virtual land parcels and other in-game NFT products on decentralized virtual reality platforms including Decentraland, The Sandbox, and Cryptovoxels.

Decentraland's LAND is permanently owned by the group, giving players complete ownership of their virtual properties and creations. Given Gen Z's experience with virtual worlds and how their understanding of valuable assets varies from that of previous generations, virtual world assets provide them with the versatility and option that they value: "

5. Properties and documentation from the real world

Real-world properties such as property and bonds, and documents such as credentials, licenses, medical records, birth and death certificates, can be tokenized.

However, this category is still in its early stages of growth, with few applications but, as the crypto world and NFTs grow and expand, who's to say you won't be able to own a vineyard in another country thousands of miles away one day (perhaps soon)? Your digital wallet can soon contain proof of every certificate, license, and asset you own, for all we know.

74

CHAPTER 15

PROBLEMS OR CONTROVERSIES SURROUNDING NFTS AND CRYPTOART

In the NFT market, there's no money to be made. However, you might have heard that NFTs are the subject of some debate, especially regarding their effect on the environment.

Artists may contribute by attempting to produce carbon-neutral artwork (Beeple has already promised to do this going forward as the above tweet explains). However, because of the way cryptocurrency systems are constructed, the problem is even more severe.

To keep its users' financial records safe, Ethereum, Bitcoin, and other cryptocurrencies depend on a 'proof-of-work mechanism (similar to a complex series of puzzles), which consumes a tremendous amount of energy. Ethereum, in reality, consumes about the same amount of energy as the entire country of Libya. Oh, no.

ArtStation was so concerned about the effects on the environment that it recently reversed its decision to sell NFTs in the face of widespread opposition. However, organizations are working to make a difference, so it might not be as divisive in the future. Here's a look at what Blockchain for Climate is doing to help the situation.

Is it possible for someone to make an NFT?

You've made it this far, so you're probably wondering if anyone should participate. Ok, given that someone drew this Gucci Ghost (above) and sold it for an eye-watering $3,600, one would think so. Yes, legally, anyone can sell an NFT. Anyone can build work, convert it to an NFT on the Blockchain (a process is known as minting,'), and sell it in their preferred marketplace.

You can also add a commission to the file that will cost you any time anyone buys the piece, including resales. You'll need a wallet set up, as much as when buying NFTs and it'll need to be packed full of cryptocurrency and this demand for money upfront that causes the problems.

The secret fees can be exorbitant, with sites charging a 'gas' charge for each sale (the cost of the energy used to complete the transaction) and a fee for selling and purchasing. You must also account for conversion fees and price changes based on the time of day.

As a result, the payments will also be much higher than the price you get for selling the NFT. However, different sites charge different fees and some are better than others, so do your homework.

Whether or not NFTs are here to stay, they have undoubtedly become a new toy for the ultra-wealthy and there is real money to be made if you can pull it off. NFTs offer digital art a whole new significance and the prices seen at auction suggest it's a real part of the future of art and collectibles in general.

CHAPTER 16

CLIMATE-POSITIVE CRYPTOART

Non-fungible tokens (NFTs) have been hailed as a panacea for everything from selling il-liquid assets like real estate properties to combating counterfeiting.

Digital art, described as NFTs, can combat climate change and drive a more sustainable digital economy, according to the most recent use case being advanced. Will we look back on this time as a collective madness fueled by crypto collectors with more money than sense?

NFTs as a Constructive Power

NFTs have emerged as the solution to various problems as the environment goes digital, with virtual displacing physical. NFTs are capable of aligning rewards between fans and artists, transforming e-gaming, promoting probable scarcity, and powering a burgeoning economy for digital collectibles, according to their architects.

Can NFTs genuinely support climate change, which they are accused of exacerbating?

NFTs are directly responsible for environmental destruction, according to the statement, because they are issued and exchanged on energy-intensive blockchains that consume large quantities of electricity.

For the smart contracts used to mint and exchange, the NFTs, energy-intensive blockchains like Ethereum (though less so than bitcoin) are used, resulting in a direct carbon intensity that is climate culpable.

Not everybody believes that NFTs are the sole cause of the planet's demise. According to one group of musicians, the opposite is real. NFTs' carbon footprint has been greatly underestimated. Still, when released on low-energy blockchains, they can be a force for good, promoting a flourishing market for digital art while also offsetting carbon consumption.

The Conscience Collective, Beeple and SAF

Those who stop scouring crypto chat groups for the new 'NFT jewels' and collectives must know Beeple. One time, unknown digital artist was on his way to becoming a household name, following his work 'Everyday: The First 5000 Days' sold at Christie's for a record $69.3 million. As a result, Beeple became the third most expensive living artist to be sold at the auction.

Beeple is collaborating alongside numerical performers such as Andres Resigner Sara Ludy Refik Anadol and Kyle Gordon in an even more audacious NFT project: The NFT artist's collective work is being auctioned off (SAF) by the Social Alpha Foundation, a charity based on blockchain.

The revenues will go to the Open Earth Foundation (501(c)(3)), a non-profit organization committed to state-of-the-art interactive open science analysis and implementation for climate accounting following the Paris Convention. The #CarbonDrop auction in the NFT world is now trending.

The auction comprises 500 tonnes, represented by the RNDR token, with the 'Octane' parent product driving most NFT graphics. These carbon credits have been recorded as part of the program and are used to conserve the Amazon rainforest and avoid deforestation. The motive behind the environmental fundraiser is hard to criticize. Will such efforts make a major difference in combating climate change?

"It was exciting to work with these amazing artists to raise awareness about the environment and funds for critical digital public goods." Our work on global climate technology is typically highly innovative for the traditional world but not for artists, who broaden their field limits with technology,"

Investing in the prospect of low energy

Ethereum and Bitcoin have been made the world's most energy-intensive blockchains by the revenue model in which miners combine power-hungry ASICs with the crunch numbers in a race to detect new blocks and claim awards.

While much of the energy used to mine cryptocurrency is from renewable sources, proof of working blockchains is environmentally sound would be misleading. No amount of money collected from fundraisers for carbon sequestration will compensate for that. Other networks may have the key to resolving the blockchain's energy problem, especially attributed to the NFTs.

Proof of Stake, a low-energy approach to securing blockchains in which validators lock or stock assets in an intelligent contract as an incentive to ethically conduct, has been used by most blockchains that have appeared since Ethereum. If the Network Consensus Regulations apply, validators, including miners who support evidence of work chains, are compensated with tokens.

Ethereum is switching to Stake Evidence but this is a long and complicated process. In the meantime, miners continue to carry out trillions of calculations per second to protect the Ethereum network through proof of work.

It was still hard to convince crypto users to turn to low-energy alternatives. Users, however, now have a more tangible incentive to turn to Stake Proof chains: money. Simply stated, the use of Ethereum is prohibited.

Demand for block space, powered by Defi and NFTs, has increased gas prices to ever highs. Proof of stake chains previously dormant or under construction is starting to gain traction as retail customers payout online purchases that now reach $100 per transaction regularly.

The most popular of these is Polygon (formerly Matic), a low-cost and scalable blockchain connecting to the Ethereum network. Polygon's decentralized application ecosystem (dApps) has proved a fertile breeding ground for low-energy, low-cost NFTs.

Hundreds of NFT-focused companies have set up a shop on Polygon, many of the buildings into the metavers of Decentraland –

a user-owned virtual universe. The latter include TradeStars, Combat Racers, and Decentral Games, with virtual casinos that can be visited worldwide.

Tezos is another intelligent contract chain that benefited from the focus on the energy bill of Ethereum. Mike Tyka, an AI artist, has selected Tezos to launch his NFT collection citing Proof of Stake's environmental credentials.

"Mining Ethereum-based NFTs will spare years of trying to minimize my climate impact by just one button" Tyka, who has a doctorate in biophysics and is aware of the need to promote sustainability, hypothesized. "After hearing about a few suggested alternatives, I decided to embrace what I believe is the only practical and ethical future for NFTs if I want to enter the vacuum.

The digital artist has also shown interest in other NFT marketplaces focused on PoS.

As projects finding a way out of Ethereum's high costs step towards the proof of stake systems like Polygon and Tezos and users follow suit, the energy dilemma of NFTs can only disappear.

Digital enthusiasts are eager to trade the latest NFTs but hundreds of dollars are unwilling to pay for this right. With Stake chains proof, you can get the best of both worlds: low fees and collaboration on climate change.

Use modern technologies to fix old issues

The idea of a blockchain that allows environmental changes can seem far-reaching, if not ludicrous. After all, a quinquennial event scheduled to begin in 2023 is the Paris Agreement and its net zero-emission route independent of non-state actors such as corporations and subnational governments.

The Open Earth Foundation seeks to complement GST by supporting a new methodology – NFTs – by active people in solving an old issue. As a result, affluent art collectors and celebrities will indulge in the trendy new NFT craze while contributing to carbon mitigation and climate accountability.

Naturally, self-awareness is important to recognize everyday habits that lead to climate change. In that regard, NFT and crypto stakeholders will be encouraged to minimize their carbon footprint as much as possible through a public awareness campaign lasting months.

Beeple already declared that his future work would be carbon-neutral or negative and that NFT platforms, artists, and even customers are likely to follow as environmental pressures increase. This may include carbon credits, a commitment to more energy-efficient blockchains, and financial incentives for artists who create neutral carbon work, etc.

NFTs are still in their infancy, still accounting for a small percentage of all Ethereum transactions in the context of advertising. Given the industry's immaturity, it is encouraging that efforts are still made to implement healthy environmental practices.

Perhaps we need to thank sensitive musicians or perhaps the NFT craze draws attention to the long-standing question of energy usage in the blockchain.

CHAPTER 17

THE REAL DOWNSIDES OF NFTS AND CRYPTOCURRENCY

Art Theft

You may have seen the Twitter blocklists to prevent the tokenization of your work. This is particularly true in hyper-capitalist economies, where there is little or no oversight and it's a free-for-all. It's a serious problem that's putting many artists' careers in jeopardy.

In the same way, that trust cannot be replaced in the real world, trust cannot be replaced in NFTs. The fundamental bridge required to persuade others that you are trustworthy and can be trusted with their money is confidence.

There are already marketplaces like SuperRare and Nifty that demand multiple authentication layers before allowing artists to list their work. However, there are still many flaws, as other sites like Rarible and Opensea allow everyone to upload work, allowing thieves to steal content and benefit.

Manipulation/Money Laundering

I've been reading a lot about how Cryptoart can be used to launder money. It's real and there's nothing you can do about it. While many digital artists are outraged, fine artists are well aware that this has been going on for centuries in the real world.

That isn't to suggest that there aren't real collectors who want to buy cool art, but it's unknown how much money is used to collect art versus laundering money genuinely.

A recent uproar erupted over the $69 million sales of Beeple's work, which cemented his status as the world's third-most successful living artist but may have exposed a nefarious underhanded scheme.

Crime and Blockchain

Criminals have only passed on from the last non-traceable currency) to the next non-traceable currency (crypto) (crypto). For decades, people have used cash to commit tax fraud, make drug deals and launder money.

I'm sure we've all heard of the drug war, but people still use them regardless of your position. To execute drug deals in the past, you had to meet up in person. This made it very risky since there was a much higher chance of being hurt or duped. On the dark web, cryptocurrency enables online marketplaces to work similarly to free markets, except for narcotics.

These markets work like every other online marketplace — reviews, storefronts, and so on — but they eliminate any of the risks of meeting in person because the orders will be delivered and your money will be sent automatically, with no risk of the chargeback (Once bitcoin is sent, you cannot return it).

Business instability

Given its meteoric rise, Bitcoin has a long history of being volatile. Its value fluctuates by the second and while this is valid for almost every currency since it isn't commonly used and is often valued on speculation, there's no way of knowing what it's worth. It could happen today, tomorrow, next week, next month, or even now and it has in the past.

Its uncertainty is treated as an asset (like a stock) rather than tangible capital for tax purposes. There are some claims to be made that when large companies invest in it, the capital will end uprising at the top — but crypto as a whole is now largely decentralized and spread out to the point that no single organization has a majority share.

The only way that could happen is if large mining farms or institutions banded together and pooled their money, but that is highly unlikely considering how dispersed the industry is and how each group has its vested interests.

Contrary viewpoints

I believe it is important to discuss how to combat the negatives since, as we have learned, cryptocurrencies and NFTs are unlikely to go away, so you must be prepared.

Combating ArtTheft

There are already groups of artists who are afraid of being tokenized if they post their work online; however, it has never prevented people from printing your work and selling it at conventions (which many of my friends have personally fallen victim to).

Should conferences, then, be outlawed?

No, and, like conferences, NFTs are yet another marketplace where the more legitimized it becomes, the more you as an artist will need to learn how to protect your work and keep it out of the wrong hands.

I'm not saying you should just embrace this thievery, but it'll just worsen as long as the world continues to follow this new form of economy. However, the more legitimized it becomes, the more governed it will become.

The current platforms that uphold a verification process (Nifty, Raible, SuperRare, and so on) are well-established and growing. There's also the fact that true collectors will only want to buy from reputable vendors.

It's the same thing that happens when a trained art historian verifies an original 18th-century painting's authenticity. Large corporations may also partner with organizations to release their properties as a confirmed brand.

There is also debate about the ramifications of copyright legislation. Large media conglomerates (Disney, Marvel, etc.) may (or already have) become interested in this space, making it much more critical that artists have the necessary knowledge to navigate this new terrain. The next time you create work, bear in mind that it can be included in the NFT room, and be aware of your rights in that space.

Fighting all of this as an artist is exhausting. I see your point. We're constantly up against tshirt bots on Twitter, Etsy pirates, convention art thieves, Instagram reposters, and even large corporations like Urban Outfitters stealing our jobs and now this.

Since the dawn of time, criminals and con artists have existed. Although they have invaded the NFT room, you must know how to defend yourself as a digital creative. Many artists already use techniques such as watermarks, low-res copies, anti-distribution provisions in the event of a complaint, etc.

You may also ban any account you suspect of stealing artwork. Unfortunately, this is unlikely to be sufficient, as the rate at which bot accounts can be generated outpaces your ability to control them.

That is all the more justification why artists must advocate for better platforms and technological advancements to protect our work. All of this suggests that this is not a direct negative of NFT technology and we as artists must put pressure on existing outlets to counteract it.

Money Laundering

One thing to keep in mind is that if you plan to put your work up yourself, you will receive 100% of the money (and all the following royalties). While the other party might be eligible to use it as a tax deduction, the money from the transaction goes to you.

Multi-layered schemes (such as the allegations surrounding Beeple) in which an individual lists a piece of work and then bids on it as if they were two separate parties are the most troubling cases of money laundering. This, on the other hand, has little effect on you and, in fact, increases the value of your work when people invest in ETH/NFTs.

Another thing to remember is that the vast majority of cryptoartists and collectors truly believe in the idea of NFTs and want it to succeed. This entails legitimizing it as a legitimate marketplace and purchasing/speculating in the same way that a real-world marketplace does.

There are many genuine art enthusiasts out there who genuinely want to collect cool art. Similarly, most artists are genuine artists who simply want to share and sell their work. They are aware of money laundering and, like you, are likely to hate it.

I'd also like to point out that banks are responsible for a large portion of money laundering in the fine art world (which is likely to move to NFTs). The FinCEN files revealed many of this and it's a big subject that everybody should be aware of. Many businesses and banks set up "shell companies," which effectively operate as a separate agency to move money under a legal transaction's pretext.

Another major explanation for the importance of cryptocurrency/NFTs is that they avoid fraud since all transactions are registered and cannot be tampered with on a blockchain network.

Decentralization prevents all of the money from accumulating in the wrong hands.

CHAPTER 18
ENVIRONMENTAL ISSUES WITH CRYPTOART

Cryptoart is a piece of metadata (generally, an image or connection to an image/file, the file's author, date stamps, related contracts or text, and the piece's buyer) that is attached to a "coin" (which has monetary value on a marketplace) and stored in a blockchain.

An NFT is a one-of-a-kind piece of cryptoart. You may think of each NFT as a collectible or trading card with its value, which is influenced by the overall market value of NFTs, the Ethereum network, and cryptocurrency in general. Without the beans, they're like beanie babies.

Cryptoart is purchased and sold with and its value is measured in, Ethereum, a 6-year-old cryptocurrency that was trading at 1 ETH = \$1476.21 at the time of writing (2 pm March 2nd, 2021).

Some artists have written about the unique environmental costs of cryptoart. The precise amount of energy used to mint artwork on the blockchain varies but ranges from weeks to months to years (and in some cases decades) of a typical EU or US citizen's energy usage. (At cryptoart. wtf, you can see how much energy each NFT uses and emits.)

This kind of gleeful wastefulness is a crime against humanity during unparalleled temperature rises, sea-level rise, widespread species extinction, the complete loss of permanent sea ice, endless extreme weather events, and all the other hallmarks of total climate collapse.

While accounts vary on the degree to which NFTs are specifically contributing to the issue, there isn't much disagreement that "powering an art market with incredible quantities of burned oil" is a bad thing. However, regardless of your general feeling that "okay, there are some bad parts," if you received this article, it might be because you asked a question like this:

But can cryptoart help us solve our ecological problems?

Is it only worth stopping because of the energy costs while other crypto type parts are useful?

Is crypto type detrimental to the environment just as art fairs and physical products are?

Can the cryptoart market instead be fuelled with offsets and renewable energy?

Isn't it a good idea to allow individual artists to sell their work?

There is nothing special about the energy cost of cryptoart and does not apply to something that can be "minted" or purchased and sold with a currency based on the burning of fossil fuels in the Ethereum blockchain.

What's the reason?

This is because major cryptocurrencies, especially Bitcoin and

Ethereum (with which NFTs are being traded), use the 'proof of work protocol to assess their value.

In essence, job evidence is a way to ensure that "the prover" has made the necessary calculation effort (the system doing a task). The definition was designed in 1993 to deter spam and bots. Evidence was meant for average users to be invisible, but that makes things like launching a denial-of-service attack difficult. It's a little puzzle version of the machine.

Until 2009, when evidence was used to establish the Bitcoin digital currency (in conjunction with another technology known as the blockchain, a type of public ledger). Bitcoin "miners" use special machines to solve proof of work puzzles and compete to verify blocks on the blockchain for Bitcoin. to create a bitcoin.

If the solution is fine, which is very rare, the miner receives a new coin. The more a computer "plays," the more competitive it becomes. Consider it a gamble, with a ticket per kilowatt-hour. Mining is this procedure's tag.

In 2009, mining started innocently as a background process that could run on a laptop while it was idle. On the other hand, the blockchain's mining blocks' sophistication is designed to develop over time. This is because the relative rate of newly mined coins remains constant as the network grows (for Bitcoin, about 1 block is mined every 10 minutes).

The evidence of work jigsaw becomes harder to solve the problem of further computer mining. Miners are improving GPUs and more computers. The puzzles are getting more complex. Miners switch to low-cost power areas. The puzzles are getting more complex. Warehouses are upgraded and containers are air-conditioned. The puzzles are getting more complex.

After a decade in which the cryptocurrency sector is rapidly growing, we now have a financial network that consumes more capital than Argentina, without a regulatory structure or federal supervision. This is not a new issue; the environmental damage caused by a proof-of-work out-of-control was known for as long as there was crypto-currency.

Unless you assume that we are talking about intangible, this devastation has a measurable, outsourced cost: according to a recent study by the University of New Mexico, each $1 of bitcoin value resulted in a loss of $0.49 in health, climate, and losses to the USA in 2018.

The current ecological costs of cryptotyping and cryptocurrency are very real and very high. While measures can be taken to control energy expenses, the crypto-market still relies on a value system that essentially binds worth spending physical resources. This partnership is not undone, no matter how low the cost of mint tokens is or the proportion of green energy.

A value system that can only understand itself as to what has been burnt materially to produce investments up to now and what will materially need to be burned tomorrow is unsustainable for the future we have to create, which has decoupled value with waste, where labor units are not purchased and sold for wages.

Also, the remaining qualities of the crypto type are profoundly troubling.

Cryptoart reworks digital artworks mainly as tokens of currency, material, and ideas secondary to a market value asset.

Cryptoart generates artificial scarcity for digital products, generating an 'original' that can be owned for resale purposes.

Cryptoart re-creates some of the worst elements of current art markets, creating the superstardom of those who have had success or already wealth and ties to the realities of many those who will see no such return.

Cryptoart has no intellectual property rights. No legal mechanism exists to prohibit entry into and selling copyright materials as NFTs, with or without the author's permission or the copyright holder. If an NFT has been minted, the blockchain or secondary market will no longer be withdrawn.

Cryptotype of smart contracts does not have a legal defense. Any talk of NFT contracts "requiring resales to cut the artist" or "compensating gallery staff" is wholly dependent on the buyer's goodwill.

Cryptoart enables a few early artists to become wealthy from a scheme designed for rewarding investors, not artists.

The fully functioning value structure of a fully functioning NFT economy is reprehensible. We can't let it go. The only way is to refuse this whole towel. No "my plant is solar," or "we plant for each coin a tree," or "we move to proof of interest" or "we are liable to have a less destructive NFT" or "the viable alternative is my smart contract."

This is ultimate liberalism, a reformist mentality that thinks that if we can address the worst problems, eliminate the bad apples, get better regulatory systems in place - then the system can only operate rather than internalize the system which often causes harm based on fundamentally broken, hateful, hyper-capitalist paradigm.

The only realistic alternative is complete moral refusal. Anything less (sell, collect, post links with NFT artists, yes even try to find a less ecologically devastating model) retains this site's worst sections' influence. It grants a moral gray-zone— "Oh, maybe it's not so bad if my favorite artist is involved?" Or "but I know this person cares and contributes to the world- maybe they know something I don't do?"

I am well aware of the desperation of trying to survive in a world that has underestimated and underestimated the arts and how convincing a vision of escape can be.

I just want to see a world, which rewards artists for their work without requiring them to put their wellbeing, security, and artistic integrity at risk. This isn't just my political conviction; it's a desire that benefits me and those I love directly. It's a future I must believe in every day.

Nevertheless, we have to do this by collective ownership and strong social programs, such as universal basic income, universal health care, divestiture from war and police operations, a controlled property market that does not benefit from housing shortages and rents, worker's unions, food services, environmental security, and real wealth taxes.

It is not an individualist fantasy of a pyramid scheme that makes investors reward artists and thieves directly from our common future.

Many would call me unreal and naïve, unable to sacrifice the world we are experiencing today due to our idealist vision of tomorrow; and I would like to suggest to them that we have invented an extra-sovereign monetary system that has produced billions of dollars and is kept back by energy consumption in a small country within ten years.

CHAPTER 19

NFT & CRYPTOART: BUBBLE OR REVOLUTION?

The interest in NFTs and Cryptoart has exponentially increased in recent months. The art market is usually inaccessible to common citizens because of the absurd nature of such pieces. What if you could purchase just a portion of the property and share it with others? Tokenization is feasible.

Tokenization is the development of blockchains of a fungible token representing the underlying asset and its value. Tokenizing can revolutionize creative disciplines, including the art sector.

So, why do art tokenize?

The benefit of using this method is that every asset can be digitized while ensuring that its transmission between various owners is smooth. Two NFTs will never be the same and interchangeable, each with special features that distinguish it.

A Bound Bubble To Burst

First reaction (very common):

Why would someone buy cryptography, far less spending millions on something just a JPEG file?

First of all, NFTs and Cryptoart must not be confused. Even though they are closely related, they are two different things.

Cryptoart refers to art using the technology of blockchain.

It's a modern digital art category. This description is very general and very logical since the discipline is relatively new and the complexities and borders of this art have not yet been determined.

Cryptoart booms with modern digital aesthetics, offering a solution to the challenge to unauthorized people who copy their work to artists and depreciate them. A conceptual artist who pushes the cryptoart limits.

NFT is a blockchain technology characteristic specified according to the ERC-721 (non-smooth digital assets) and ERC-1155 (semi-smooth assets) Ethereum specifications. The main properties of NFTs are:

indivisible (not fractional), verifiable (a unique identifier that specifies who owns NFTs), and indestructible (cannot be destroyed or removed). NFTs may include any digital material including sketches, graffiti, animated GIFs, songs, or video game objects. NFTs in the blockchain world are the next big deal.

Cryptoart can easily be seen as a bubble, but I don't believe that. It's not my opinion alone. This has already been seen on the market with the most famous artists globally, including Banksy and Beeple, for $69 million. The overall value of NFT trade in 2020 amounted to 250 million dollars, 299% up on the previous year, and continues to rise in 2021.

Why do we take care of this?

Many people who participated in NFTs in the early stages and started trade saw great returns. Still, we've formally entered the cyberpunk era with a fully digitalized society and the art world is heading for NFTs already and this is just the start.

NFTs generate digital scarcity of which none existed before. It doesn't matter if you can, for example, screenshot them. Consider this: is Van Gogh's perfect reproduction worth the same amount as the original?

However, what makes NFT art great? The Crypto Era

Why do many observers use the Internet in their metaphors of Crypto World?

Our digital networks, built to enhance our basic connectivity, can change anything and the blockchain causes a revolution, yes. It looks like they kill the old and start something new.

NFTs will capture and appreciate the spirit of this generation in the future. That's what makes NFTs relevant. It was not, however, a revival. One of the main reasons people have become a possible alternative to NFTs is the absence of numerical scarcity in the creative economy. The curiosity has gone up.

Creators of Economy

It's hard to track the buyers who fuel this craze. NFTs can also manage the license agreement process when integrated explicitly with blockchain technology. The decentralized existence of NFTs is an important factor in providing the creator economy with vital digital capital.

For example, if a buyer of one of the parts sold it, the buyer keeps 10% of the original purchase price. Notice that there can be an infinite number of NFTs. Each creator's case of usage determines the number of copies generated. NFTs can also manage the license agreement process when integrated explicitly with blockchain technology.

Falls and difficulties

In reality, NFT is far from user-friendly and open to the public, even worse. In certain instances, you must set up an Ethereum wallet and use it, buy products and pay transaction fees during the purchase of NFTs.

Generally, people fear that we are in the midst of a bubble and the appeal NFTs have created in recent years will easily vanish. NFTs are expected to be old-fashioned speculative activities for the near future by many observers.

Eventually, new ways to infringe copyright have arisen, but artists can still make more money on the Internet. New forms of piracy come with a new form of land. This is a new challenge.

Regulation

Since the NFTs continues to be a relatively recent invention, no clear legal framework exists around them. Still, they are governed by national and international law but regulators are working on these systems and they are coming soon. Some countries in Europe have released ICO-related guidelines or regulations, including Switzerland, Germany, Estonia, and Malta.

The NFT can be added to the digital token. It's a digitally intangible asset that reflects one or more rights: the NFT has its worth. The owners may be identified and the pseudonyms or addresses used are attached.

But should we legally regard CryptoPunks or CryptoKitties as a work of art?

The issue is complicated. It is very difficult to include them in this group or to exclude them. It is difficult to include them since the NFT box is in a category separate from the listed works. Since the law develops and the concept of work is highly subjective, it is difficult to exclude them.

The NFT space will allow creators to capture a greater share of the profits of everything they generate and sell. If creators use an institution to distribute their material, they receive only a small part of the benefit. Book writers signing agreements with big publishers or artists with record labels are the clearest example of this.

NFTs have exploded with designers, artists, and musicians around the world who embrace digitally exclusive tokens. If broadly applied, NFTs could be a transformer of digital scarcity. NFT mania has the potential in many respects and in many sectors to overcome previously unresolvable problems.

In recent years on-Fungible Tokens (NFTs) captured titles with the sale of artists including pop star Grimes and EDM creator 3LAU in millions of dollars. As part of the Crypto Kitties, NFTs joined the market in 2017, a blockchain game that uses digital cat collectibles.

However, in October last year, Christie's New York Art Auction House made history by selling the first-ever NFT related to physical artwork — Portraits of a Mind: Block 21, sale over $130,000 by London-based artist Benjamin Gentilli. Since then, the popularity of NFTs has increased rapidly.

Another record-breaking NFT job was auctioned off at Christie's, this time strictly digitally, for a current $3.25 million bid. This has resulted in an increase in NFTs' overall market capitalization to over $350 million in just six months.

CONCLUSION

NFTs have unlimited potential and possibilities and recent record sales help the technology progress. One of the current barriers to widespread adoption is the lack of widespread awareness about the crypto world and blockchain technology. "If you teach people to taste it, allow them to experience it, they won't be overwhelmed by it," said the creator John G Fields, Develop Your Base.

Security is part of this training since new users in the Blockchain area need to know how to secure their wallets and private keys to prevent hackers from being exposed to their valuable digital assets.

Many digital artifacts, collectibles, and investments, which will undoubtedly be devastating, are highly valuable because of their rareness and rarity. Developers and creators must ensure that strong copyright and licensing are entered into intelligent contracts to ensure digital assets' integrity.

The majority of currently available crypto wallets are extremely complex and hard to use for inexperienced users and mainstream beginners. Wallets like Coinbase Wallet, Pillar Wallet Enjin Wallet, or WAX Wallet (WCW), to name but a few, are nevertheless constantly being developed and published to improve this.

NGRAVE ZERO is another wallet to keep an eye on since it is the "coldest" and most secure crypto wallet that is also incredibly user-friendly and seamless to be used. ZERO's high-quality tactile screen not only provides a safe and secure environment where users store and exchange their virtual properties; it also has the interesting potential to allow owners to show their virtual collectors and assets from a tiny, portable device to others.

Another part of mass education is to see how geeky, nerdy, and scientific NFTs and blockchain technology remain. Further simplification will be essential so that people who are not familiar with blockchain can easily use and understand it.

Dr. Jesse Reich (CEO Splinterlands) explains how the challenge "is in rendering blockchain invisible to an inexperienced user while accessible to an advanced user." in the board The Future of Gaming & Non-Fungible Tokens.

While projects such as CryptoKitties successfully launched new blockchain users and growth and increased NFT use cases in recent months, a long way remains to be gone. The passion of NFTs is mainly in the gaming, art, and collectibles niche fields, but new enterprises increasingly broaden NFTs into other aspects of our physical existence.

We can see how NFTs become transférable between different worlds, virtually and physically alike as more major brands enter the battlefield (such as Nike, which has licensed shoes such as NFTs, called CryptoKicks, that enable users to 'breed.' As CEO of Animoca Brands Yat Siu puts it so aptly:

"How many game companies will say, let's use those Nike shoes in our virtual games?" if millions of people have virtual Nike shoes unexpectedly. Yat Siu, CEO of Animoca Brands

As more people become aware of the value and potential that NFTs can offer, more major brands, big investors, and risk capital firms take notice and become interested. The co-founders of Morgan Creek Digital, Anthony Pompliano, and Jason Williams, have made a "great gamble" on digital art NFTs that outperform the physical art market.

Because of their exceedingly long product lifecycles and their willingness to offer various monetization models, Indie blockchain game designers have started drawing venture capital. New governance tokens in the NFT sector, as they were in the Defi sector, are creating interest and there is no evidence of the exciting new NFT and Defi types.

However, the way ahead for NFTs is not barrier-free, as they will face potential regulatory hurdles. The crypto space is still very young and needs to continue as a community by producing many new projects despite their coming and going projects.

Thanks for reading.